DIY Lipstick: How to Make Lipstick from Scratch

Chloe Taylor

Liability Disclaimer

Although every precaution has been taken to verify the accuracy of the information contained herein, the author assumes no responsibility for any errors or omissions. No liability is assumed for damages that may result from the use of the information contained within.

Thank you so much for purchasing this book! I hope that you enjoy the book and the recipes that are included.

What's New

This book covers two simple lipstick bases, including a vegan option. There are also five different color recipes that cover the most popular shades of lipstick. Of course there are step-by-step instructions included AND suppliers to get you started in making homemade cosmetics!

Table of Contents

What to Get

Before thinking about how beautiful your lipstick will look, you need to know what tools and suppliers you can source all of your ingredients from. When it comes to finding the ingredients you will need for your lipstick, you can find those products at JustPigments.com and TKBTrading.com. These suppliers were chosen because of their vast array of pigments and low shipping costs. (*Note: I am not affiliated with any of these companies and will not receive compensation for recommending them.*)

For the recipes in this book you will need:

-     beeswax (or candelilla wax for the vegan alternative),

- carnauba wax,

- jojoba oil,

- castor oil,

- and shea butter.

You can switch out some of the ingredients or add to the recipe, but we will discuss this in detail later.

Below is a suggested list of items you can find already in your kitchen, Amazon.com, or your local store.

Tools

- Grinder of your choice (explained in more detail below)

- Glass or Stainless Steel Stirrer

- Glass Beaker or Measuring Cup

- Stainless Steel Measuring Spoons

- Face Masks

- Disposable Gloves

- Hair Net

- Sauce Pan

- Alcohol (91%)

- Wax Paper

- Lip Balm or Lipstick Tubes with

Lipstick Mold

- Stove

- Apron or Old Clothes

Choosing a Grinder

A grinder will be needed if you plan to use iron

oxides – matte pigments that make lipstick opaque.

Here are a few of the most popular choices ranging

from least to most expensive:

Electric Herb Grinder: An inexpensive choice since it is priced under $10. These grinders are perfect for very small batches of two grams or less. A couple of drawbacks from using these are that the pigments can stick to the sides of the container, and that the device uses batteries.

Coffee Grinder: Another inexpensive option usually priced around $20. Coffee grinders are great for bigger batches and they blend the pigments really well. Be aware that the motors of coffee grinders tend to burn out from being overworked and from powders seeping into the motor compartment.

Food Processor: These are usually priced at $40 and up! They are a good choice for big batches, they blend pigments extremely well, and they are designed to run for a long time.

If you plan to use a coffee grinder or food processor, make sure to use it for makeup only.

Setting Up

Once you're ready to begin, make sure to sanitize your workplace, your tools, and the lip packaging you plan to use. Use the wax paper to cover the workplace for an easy cleanup process.

Ingredients to Know

If this is your first time working with raw materials, it can be an overwhelming process. I've put a list of the basic color additives that you may come across.

Micas – These are colorful powders that add sheen and shimmer to lipsticks. They require no grinding or sifting to use.

Iron Oxides – These are matte pigments that can be used to add depth, and opacity to your lipstick. They only come in a few colors namely black, red, and yellow. The black iron oxide can have a blue or brown undertone, and the red iron oxide can have a blue or yellow undertone. It is important to know these nuances when color mixing, because they can make your lipstick morph into an entirely different color. Iron oxides require some sifting or grinding before use.

Ultramarines – These are also matte pigments and include purple, pink, and blue colors. **THESE CANNOT BE USED IN LIPSTICKS!**

FD&C and D&C colorants – These powders have a bigger color range including multiple variances of yellow, and red. These are sheer and have to be used with iron oxides to get maximum payoff. There are some that cannot be used in lipsticks. **Please see the U.S. Food and Drug Administration's "Color**

Additives Permitted for Use in Cosmetics" for the

most up-to-date information.

The Base

A basic lipstick consists of oils, waxes, and color additives. Depending on the lipstick you want to make, the percentages of each component will vary. Cream lipsticks tend to have at least 50% oil content, while matte lipsticks have less. The recipes below are for a cream lipstick base, since from experience most people enjoy using a moisturizing lipstick that has great color payoff and a hint of sheen. They both make approximately 1 cup of lipstick base.

Cream Lipstick Base

> 2 ¼ tsp. Shea Butter
>
> 1 tbsp. plus 1 tsp. Carnauba Wax
>
> 2 tbsp. Beeswax Wax
>
> 6 tbsp. plus 1½ tsp. Castor Oil

5 tbsp. plus 2 tsp .Jojoba Oil

Cream Lipstick Base (Vegan Alternative)

2 ¼ tsp. Carnauba Wax

1 tbsp. plus 2 tsp. Candelilla Wax

1 tbsp. plus 2 tsp. Shea Butter

6 tbsp. plus 1½ tsp. Castor Oil

5 tbsp. plus 2 tsp. Jojoba Oil

The above lipstick bases include ingredients that all have at least a one year shelf life. If you choose to use ingredients with a short shelf-life, it will shorten the life of your product. The carnauba wax offers the benefit of a higher melting point, so it decreases the chances of your lipstick melting due to sun exposure. Candelilla wax also gives the benefit of a higher melting point, while also providing a glossy finish and helping the color adhere to the lips. Beeswax is used to assist with the rigidity of the product and help the lipstick stay on the lips. Shea butter is a great moisturizer and helps the lipstick maintain its rigidity without adding an enormous amount of wax. Castor oil provides a glossy look and its high viscosity gives the lipstick a creamy feel, while jojoba oil provides moisturizing benefits.

If you plan to switch out any ingredients, it is extremely important to switch it out for something with a consistency that is close to the current ingredient. For instance, if you are opposed to using Shea Butter, switch it out for a butter that has a texture close to it. Cocoa butter would not be a good substitute in this instance, because it will make the lipstick extremely hard and more likely to break.

Now let's put the base together!

Directions: While you are heating a pot of water, put the amount of wax you plan to use inside of a glass container. Once the water starts to simmer, insert the glass into the pot of water. Allow the wax to completely melt but not boil. Add your oils and melted butters. Use your stirrer to mix your ingredients thoroughly. Turn off the burner and take your glass container out of the sauce pan. Transfer your ingredients to a heat safe container, and store it in a cool dry place or in the refrigerator.

The Color

Dyes, pigments, micas, and a host of other colors that are derived from natural sources can be used in your lipstick. As mentioned before, there are some color additives you **cannot** use on the lips, such as chromium oxides and ultramarines. **Please see the U.S. Food and Drug Administration's "Color Additives Permitted for Use in Cosmetics" for the most up-to-date information.**

Before you start to create colors, you may want to study a bit of color theory. This will help you tremendously as it will explain all of the obstacles that may arise when creating colors. Use a site like TryColors.com to practice your color mixing.

Let's make some colors for our lipsticks. Here are 5 shades you can try!

Beautiful Nightmare – a deep berry lipstick

> 1 tbsp. Red Oxide (blue shade)

> 1 tbsp. Manganese Violet

Candyland – a baby pink lipstick

> ½ tbsp. Carmine

> 1½ tbsp Titanium Dioxide

That's Hot – an orange lipstick

> ¼ tsp. Red Oxide (red shade)

> 1 tbsp. FD&C Red #40

> 1 tbsp. FD&C Yellow #5

Mrs. Peterson – a mauve lipstick

> 1 tbsp. Red Oxide (blue shade)

> 1 tbsp. Red Oxide (red shade)

1 tbsp. Titanium Dioxide

Natural – a pinkish brown based nude

½ tbsp. Brown Oxide

1 tbsp. Pearl Mica

1 tbsp. Titanium Dioxide

When making a lipstick color, grind iron oxides for at least two minutes. The longer you grind, the less likely the color will come out streaky, and the more vibrant the color becomes.

Creating the Product

Finally, we are getting to the part where we create our lipstick! Before we get started, it's important to follow the instructions in "The Basics" section to set up your work area.

Now let's get started!

For lip balm tubes:

1. Scoop out about 1 tablespoon of base for each lipstick you want to make.

2. Twist the lip balm tubes all the way down.

3. Melt the base over low heat.

4. Add the amount of color additives to reach the desired opacity and stir thoroughly.

5. Pour the mixture into the lip balm tube. Once it cools it will shrink in the middle, so save the remainder to pour the rest onto the top.

For lipstick molds:

1. Take the lightest oil you are using in your recipe and use a cotton swab to grease each cavity in the mold you plan to use.

2. Scoop out about 1½ tablespoons for each lipstick you want to make.

3. Melt the base over low heat.

4. Add the amount of color additives to reach the desired opacity and stir the mix thoroughly.

5. Pour the mixture into the lipstick mold cavity, then store it in the freezer for 30 minutes.

6. Once you take it out of the freezer, scrap the excess product off the top of the mold. You can either dispose it or save it and remelt it.

7. Slide the top part of the mold straight up. Do this carefully or the lipstick will break.

8. Twist the lipstick tube all the way up.

9. Slide the lipstick tube on the product until it touches the mold.

10. Lift the lipstick straight up and twist it down.

11 Tips for Creating Lipstick

1. Candelilla and carnauba wax take a while to harden, so if you're planning to switch them out, wait a few days before you finalize your recipe.

2. Try not to use castor oil at a rate greater than 50%, because the lipstick will have a greasy feel.

3. Do not overheat the ingredients, especially the butters! Butters will make your lipstick grainy if overheated.

4. Add an antioxidant like Vitamin E to help elongate the shelf life of the lipstick.

5. Do not use a large amount of iron oxides if you plan to use sparkly micas, because the mica will not show.

6. Do not grind sparkly micas, because they will lose their shimmer. Instead, hand mix them into the batch after you have finished grinding the other additives.

7. Use titanium dioxide and zinc oxide in moderation to avoid having a very draggy lipstick.

8. If you want to make a matte lipstick, consider adding a powder like kaolin in with your pigments.

9. For a more professional look, you can "flame" your lipstick. "Flaming" gives your lipstick a nice glossy appearance. Major cosmetic companies use a Bunsen burner to do this, but a hair dryer will work just fine.

10. Do not use a lot of color additives! It will make your lipstick very cakey.

11. If you have problems with your color additives sinking to the bottom, rework the steps to where you mix the color additives into a viscous oil, like castor oil, first.

F.A.Q.s

WHY IS THE COLOR NOT SHOWING ON MY LIPS?!

This happens when there is not enough iron oxide added to the base. Iron oxides coat your lips, whereas most micas will only tint your lips. Add more pigment to the base to see better results. Also, check to make sure there is not a high percentage of wax used in the formula. This can also cause the color not to show up.

HOW DO I MAKE A 24 HOUR LIPSTICK?

Long-wear lipsticks contain a delicate balance of silicones, resins, and emollients to help with their lasting ability. Some silicones have low a flashpoint which make them hazardous to work with, so take extra caution if you plan to work with them.

HOW LONG WILL MY HANDMADE LIPSTICKS LAST?

Your lipsticks will last as long as the shortest shelf life of your ingredients. For instance, if you have an oil that has a three month shelf life, your lipstick will generally last that long. The shelf life can be extended by using an antioxidant such as Vitamin E.

THE TITANIUM DIOXIDE (OR ZINC OXIDE) IS VERY CLUMPY, HOW DO I FIX THIS?

Try mixing the powders within castor oil prior to mixing it with your other ingredients. You can also buy pigments pre-dispersed in oil.

CAN I ADD ESSENTIAL OR FLAVORS OILS TO MY LIPSTICK?

You can, but make sure to research the usage levels.

Be careful of using citrus oils because they are

sensitive to light and can cause severe reactions.

CAN I USE EYESHADOW AS MY COLOR ADDITIVE?

You can, but proceed with caution. Make sure **every**

ingredient within the eyeshadow can be used on the

lips!

My Own Recipes

Made in the USA
Las Vegas, NV
29 November 2022

60652744R00020